Dabbler's Demise

For my friend Tom,

Conservation is the wellspring of nature's future and mankind's destiny.

Good hunting!

Rec Hillman
8/08

DABBLER'S DEMISE

C. Eric Hellmann

Edited by Barbara Humberger

Aventine Press

© 2007, C. Eric Hellmann
First Edition

Without limiting the rights under copyright reserved above, no part of this publication may be reproduced, stored in or introduced into a retrieval system, or transmitted, in any form or by any means (electronic, mechanical, photocopying, recording, or otherwise), without the prior written permission of both the copyright owner and the publisher of this book.

Published by Aventine Press
1023 4th Ave #204
San Diego CA, 92101
www.aventinepress.com

ISBN: 1-59330-483-8

Printed in the United States of America

ALL RIGHTS RESERVED

To my sweet Nancy.

My soft touchstone of reality, a loving partner in life's dream, a devoted mother to our handsome children, and shelter from the ravages of life's daily storms.

Epigraph

"To everything there is a season, and a time to every purpose under heaven: a time to be born, and a time to die; a time to plant, and a time to pluck up that which is planted; .... a time to get and a time to lose, a time to keep, and a time to cast away;"

            Ecclesiastes 3: 1-3, 6

Contents

Demise --- 2

Sanctuary -- 3

Sandusky Spawn --- 7

Against The Grain --------------------------------------- 12

North Shore --- 15

The Measure -- 16

New Leaf -- 17

Button -- 19

Dr. Inquisitor --- 21

Soul -- 23

Katie --- 25

Transition -- 27

Tsunamis --- 28

Kraut Kuisine --- 31

Keepers -- 33

Posted --- 35

Annie -- 37

Storm Damage -- 39

Along The Way --- 41

Frogtown -- 43

Diagnosis -- 44

Dr. Granny -- 45

Awakening --- 47

Progress --- 49

Billy Buck -- 51

Bargain -- 52

The Kiss --- 53

Connubial Conversations ----- 55

Branch ----- 57

Silent Shadow ----- 58

At Nine ----- 60

Sum Total ----- 61

Thrash'n ----- 63

Fruits Of Morpheus ----- 64

Political Planting ----- 65

Duck Watch ----- 67

God's Face ----- 69

Good Times ----- 71

It's The Truth ----- 73

From Here To There ----- 75

Sssnake ----- 77

Bedrock ---79

Silver Dowry --80

Shrine of the Miraculous Wing Shot ----------------------------------83

Mr. Lucky ---85

All ---87

Keep'n Track ---89

Nirvana --91

Living Hues ---93

Eternity --95

Season's Limit ---96

List of Illustrations

First Week of White Bass -- 4

Lattice Patios -- 6

White Bass Stringer --- 8

Below Ballville Dam -- 10

Marblehead Lighthouse --- 14

First Buck --- 18

Katie At Six Weeks --- 24

Spring Rabbit --- 30

Letchworth State Park -- 32

My Mom --- 36

Carp Catchers -- 42

Blue Flag -- 46

Afternoon Surprise --- 50

Nesting Geese ---54

Kole ---56

Mallard Moments ---62

Looking For the Season --66

Swallow On Duck Box ---68

Twilight At The Marsh ---70

Bird Dog --72

Mull Covered Bridge ---74

Oakwood Cemetery --78

Saint Hubert's Bounty ---82

John "Lucky" Kronauge ---84

Pied-billed Grebe ---88

As One --92

Toussaint Swans ---94

Foreword

I invite you to accompany me on a trek through the farm fields, coastal marshes, and the rivers of the Northwest Ohio. This is the portion of Ohio's north shore that was once the fabled Great Black Swamp which has always been an arena of historic conflict between great forces. Originally the demarcation line of the Ice Age's advance south, a place where the glaciated grove collected the melting ice pack to form Lake Erie. In Colonial times, there were great struggles of arms with the Iroquois tribes and white settlers moving west. The conflict that would follow the Revolution pitted the British and their Indian allies under Blue Jacket against the new American nation during the War of 1812. The last and most difficult conflict was when German immigrant farmers arrived to wrestle new homesteads from the bogs and meandering waterways of the rich marsh. Today the farms, marshes and green spaces are fast becoming marinas, lake condos, and homes with spacious lawns as struggling farmers face the economic realities of selling off road frontages with a view.

Federal and State government has supported and supplemented private owners and non-profit organizations to stem the loss of what was once unlimited wild space. Sadly, the days of unlimited habitat for wildlife and outdoorsmen alike has passed into history.

Acknowledgements

My special thanks to my editor, Barbara Humberger, who continues to support my literary efforts despite our discussions about how sound sometimes trumps grammar. Kudos to her placid husband, Bob, who occasionally had to act as line judge.

I must extend heart felt thanks to all my fellow hunters and conservationists at the Oak Harbor Conservation Club who have been my personal recovery staff throughout my period of disability. They always made sure there was a place for me at the table, while offering words of encouragement when life's game bag seemed empty.

I would be remiss if I did not mention my old friend, Leo Kimmet, who has been my duck blind partner for many a year. He has given me an example of quiet strength as I traverse this rocky trail to recovery. His devotion and effort insured that my attachment to Nature remained well tethered.

List of Contributors

Permission to use the photograph of the author given by Olan Mills Portrait Studios.

Permission to use the cover page photo, "Reflections – A World Turned Upside Down" was given by my friend and fellow conservationist, Ralph Burnstine of Timely Prints of Port Clinton, OH.

I would like to thank Jennifer Porter of Creative Images in Centerville, TN for her permission to use of her picture of my grandson Kole Steven Hellmann who was born 2/17/06.

Introduction

Throughout life, my emotional crutch has always been my attachment and fascination with the wild outdoors. It became my primary rhythm of life and my escape from the storm. The life scenes that played out in my early adventures in the wild formed a template that molded my inner being and influenced my future.

The poems that you sample here have also been shaded with a struggle of twelve years of physical disability, and most recently the reoccurrence of my cancer. Each day is a gift to be prized and nurtured. The experience has in many ways restricted my previously super charged life style, but on the whole has strengthened the inner me. It is my fervent hope that the caldron of adversity will refine and not destroy this human being.

In Nature all life is miraculously inter-dependent, but all God's creations are fragile and have their season.

Dabbler's Demise

Demise

  a poet, a puddle duck,
one pilgrim, one traveler,
both blown on the wing,
in real time, just dabblers.

  in search of safe harbor
from storm's stiffening winds,
trusting most to good instincts
and quiet voices within.

  both raft on the surface
but probe in the depths,
in quest of the morsel
that may extend this life yet.

  obsessed with migration
while searching things out,
one soul's go'n nowhere,
one duck's head'n south.

Sanctuary

    In lush green meadow
I've come to rest,
    To shelter from life's
tolls and quests.

    Drawn to this glade
amongst the wood,
    When daily squalls
I've scant withstood.

    The balm that Nature
does yet bequeath,
    Will heal my wounds
and set me free.

First Week of White Bass
Sandusky River Water Intake, Fremont, OH

Sandusky Spawn

Pectoral Fin

As May hemorrhages heat
they come,
Like seagulls troubling shad shoals
to sprout upon the river banks,
fast becoming channel deadfalls,
these
vagabond estuary gleaners,
these
fishermen. Not the tony catch and release anglers
of small mouth bass
nor the pothole crappie catchers
of late Summer.
Milkers of jacks and eaters of roe,
these
hunters of the flesh,
these
gatherers.

Lattice Patios
Fremont, OH Downtown Flood Wall, Sandusky River

Spiny Dorsal Fin

     Resurrected each Spring
from the dormant coals of shore-side fire rings,
they festoon the river's edge
with bird nests of tangled filament,
forked tree branch rod holders,
and on the bank relay a mosaic of broken glass.
     Lattice-work patios
of scaffolding and purloined pallets
terrace the concrete flood walls.
Construction reminiscent of frenzied termites
in pursuit of foundation caps.

Pelvic Fin

     At first blush scattered supplicants
test the run.
     With the coming of the white bass
believers eschew the trappings of Mother's Day
installing their clan matriarchs
at water's edge on folding chair thrones,
while off the bank
knots of carp genuflect
to bow and scrape upon the mudflats.

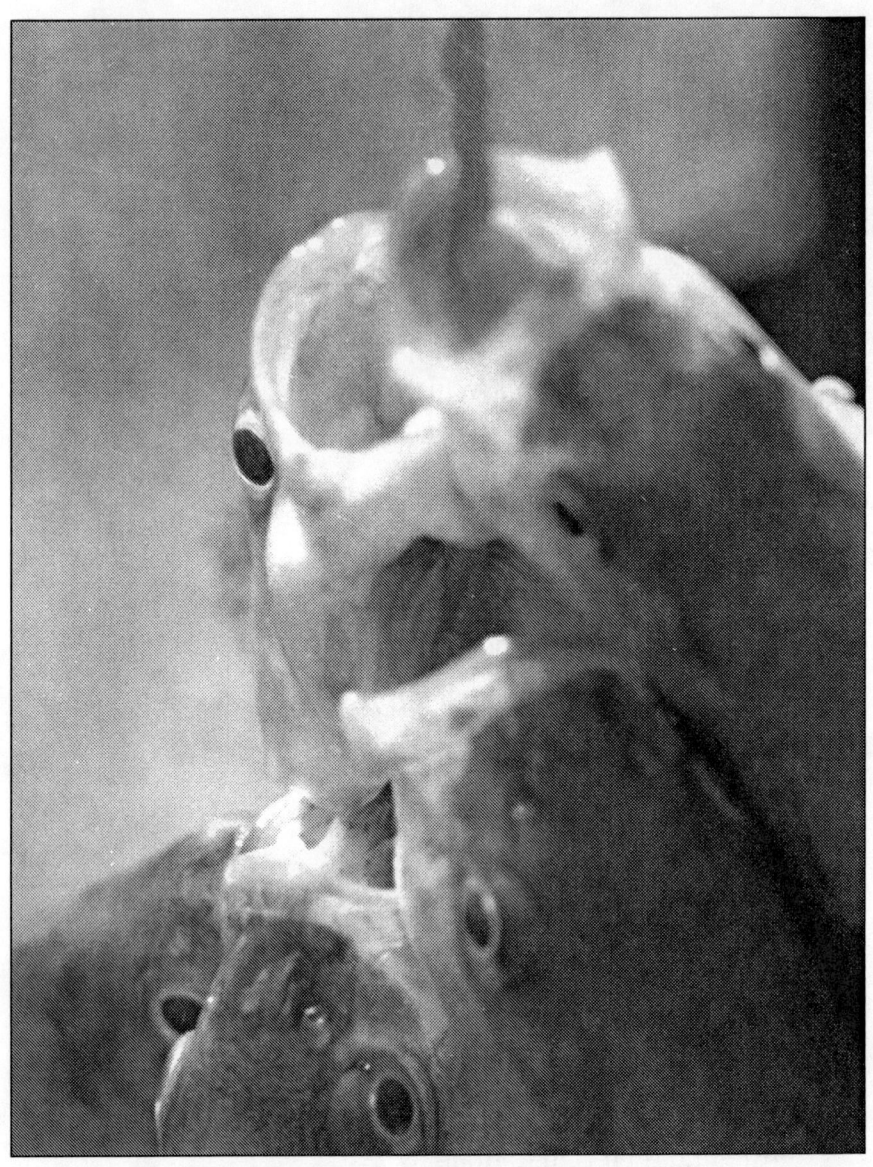

White Bass Stringer
Fremont, OH Sandusky River

Soft Dorsal Fin

     On the meandering Sandusky River
the grand finale entices
a wave of intent casters to the rapids
under the bridges of Fremont town.
Spawning walleye queuing up
among the river rocks below Ballville Dam.
     Populations change from
white bass to walleye;
from mocha to mottled.

Anal Fin

     Gone are the heady days
of treble hooks and the "big snag".
Every third man's a game warden.
     Spawners don't feed, they strike.
Many fish endure the death
of a thousand cuts
to ensure next year's cycle.
     At height of run
anglers stand shoulder to shoulder
casting wildly from the confinement of
a fisherman's scrum
which traverses the full length of the shallows.

Below Ballville Dam
Fremont, OH Sandusky River

Caudal(Tail) Fin

    The spawn abates.
Out-of-state license plates disappear
from downtown,
Fremont looses its cosmopolitan glow,
and Whitey's Diner
serves less gamey fishermen.
    Crappies and small mouth bass
recapture the locals.

Against The Grain

*Rough hewn planks
of the duck blind floor
boast substantial character and obvious age.
Byproducts
from a builder's castoff,
timbers from some forgotten barn.
Selected in haste
they provide solid support
to a stick structure of concealed intentions
and questionable longevity.
Cleaved
from native timber
and hardened with time,
these brutish planks resist nails and drill
defying motion
by sheer heft and density.
Many edges
still boast original bark
reflecting the millwright's obsession with utility,
not beauty.*

*Planks
bear exposed tunnels
restricted to a margin's edge
where termites surrendered to determined grain,
or tastier selections.
Swirling saw blade scars
are tattooed in predictable geometric regularity
that runs counter to the grain.
The dirt
and imperfections of age
are imbedded upon the once fresh hardwood
which objects not.
The floor stands solid
in contrast to the fragility
of the yellow-pine uprights
that have been thrown up to support
the deceptively camouflaged exterior.
How often
over many years
have we chosen this construction?*

Marblehead Lighthouse
Marblehead, OH

North Shore

Crouched still on limestone outcrops
At the base of Marblehead Light,
Gather'n in the summer bounty
From swaddled folds of colors bright.

Lulled into contrite submission
Adrift on Erie's soothing swells,
Watching waves lash sheltered shoreline
As the gentle breeze says all is well.

Etched in sands of ebbing eddies
Barefoot lovers leave their marks,
In the sun they stroll together,
Drifting closer after dark.

Beneath catwalk of spired lighthouse
Flows resplendent lake and gossamer bay,
Captured by the bold who'll navigate
Thrusting steel toward beacon's rays.

Gathering wealth from pummeled senses
To lay aside for future times,
Standing reluctant in departure
From Lake Erie reaches so sublime.

The Measure

It is said when reaching older age
Of all things that we've been given,
　　Most simply seem to fall away
And we face a life less driven.

　　But rarely in this world around
Do we succumb to great events,
　　More likely we've been bored to death
Ending our years as malcontents.

　　We'll be judged by stringent measures,
Not the mundane things we lack,
　　But by the depth of those who loved us,
And what we willingly gave back.

New Leaf

a sea change
from driven to given.
    approach revised
from jaded to satiated.
    attention shifted
from needed to greeted.
    condolences given
of empathy not sympathy.
    resurrected
from dismal to divine.

"with God
    all things are possible"
        Matt.19:26

First Buck
Kurt & Loren Hellmann
10/29/05

Button

Miss Loren of south Tennessee
Set aside her genteel ways,
To don fluorescent hunter's garb
And greet first season's opening day.

Stumbling in the dark black night
Along the twisting forest trails,
Long 'fore a hint of coming dawn
Slogged this bonnie lass so frail.

To scale the ladder to the heights
Of lofty deer stand perch,
She calmly claimed the waiting seat
Beside her old guide Kurt.

It took a bit of struggling
To heft that outsized gun,
Made for her by the guys
At the works of Remington.

Loren stifled great excitement
When a lone button buck appeared,
He broke cover from the tangled brush
And stretched his luck by coming near.

The deer appeared at seventy-five yards
From atop that deadly tree,
Undeterred she nailed that rambling buck
'Fore it had chance to flee.

A faultless shot delivered
That could elude the best of men,
So we're all just down-right happy
'Cause the granddaughter's only ten.

Loren's First Hunt
October 29, 2005

Dr. Inquisitor

Executioner,
tell me plain.
How many victims
have been claimed?

Roasting flesh skewed
on radiation's spit?
What time's required
before inquiry quits?

How many souls
must vile cancer take,
Rendering hides slashed and carved
to eviscerate?

Were prisoners plied
with toxic brews,
Prolonging time 'till gainful
life was through?

Have the deeds been judged
the Inquisitor's best,
Deadening brains and pain
with narcotic zest?

Were the conclusions worth
a Tinker's Darn?
Was the oath upheld
or was there only harm?

Soul

Deep in my heart there is a spring
That'll quench the needs my body brings.

But there is no point best I can tell
Where the essence of my soul does dwell.

Does it lie in skin beneath the nail?
Within my mind or composure frail?

Is it a glowing aura we all possess?
Does it ride inside our beating breasts?

Can't feel it, touch it, nor can I see,
Where in me this elusive spirit be.

But I know it's there, of that I'm sure,
One day to pass through Heaven's great door.

Katie At Six Weeks
Fremont, OH

Katie

Is it the coquettish way
she cocks her head,
or her lack of grace
when she leaves her bed?

Is it the downy coat
gathered on a spare frame,
or her nonchalance
when I call her name?

Is it her velvet ears
that I yearn to stroke,
or the love
her pug-nosed face emotes?

Is it the comic spike
that is her tail,
or those oversized paws
holding body frail?

Is it the richness of
her chocolate hide,
or her rascal nature
lurking deep inside?

A gift of the future
is what this pup's given,
life's high times and hunts
are well worth live'n.

We'll frequent the lands
of the old Erie Lake,
Ranging shore, marsh, and field
'til last hunt we take.

Transition

        tests and energy
improve.

        the unbelievable pain's
still unbelievable.

        hormone shots lubricate my female side
and mock latent machismo.

        HOT FLASH!   Freeze!   HOT FLASH!
self-incineration.

        the undesirable side effect of transition
in a woman's change of life.

        cancer is more defining!
transition to live.

Tsunamis

Piltdown Epiphany:
 Humanity's expansion will be limited to
 the number of caves available in England.

Naturalists postulate
 the soil hold seeds
 that can lie dormant for 200 years,
 awaiting only the kiss of a polished plow.

Of all the species ever produced
 over 90 % were extinct
 before mankind dropped from the trees.

Given rest,
 an asphalt byway
 will be completely reclaimed by grass.

The undertow claimed the first fruits,
 ocean bathers,
 as stranded fish flopped in vain
 on miles of unexpectedly denuded beachfront.

The Queen of the Sea
> *coasting from the Fort Railroad Station to Galle*
> *offered 800 souls as a sacrifice*
> *to elephant waves.*
Men are but high-minded fleas
> *infesting earth's hide*
> *convinced their bite will kill the host.*

At dawn on December 26, 2004 a disaster of biblical proportions unfolded in the oceans west of Aceh province in Indonesia. An earthquake of 9.0 magnitude brought death and destruction in the form of a tsunami to many countries bordering the Indian Ocean as far west as Africa. Over 160,000 people have been confirmed dead with the fear that many may be lost to the sea never to be recovered. The Queen of the Sea was a train in Sri Lanka that was traversing the coastal plain when the tsunami ripped the locomotive and eight carriage cars from the track with 1000 people aboard. An article in the Toledo Blade on January 1, 2005 tells a heartbreaking story of Nimal Premasiri who lost his wife and daughter in the disaster. They were enroute from Fort Railroad Station to Galle on the anniversary of his mother-in-law's death to feed the monks in her honor. He said he "saw waves as big as elephants coming towards us." Nimal is the station master of the 100 year old Fort Railroad Station.

Spring Rabbit
Dr. L.J. Darr Memorial Wetland
Oak Harbor, OH

Kraut Kuisine

Woodsmen cherish their old habit
of always hunting fuzzy rabbits.

Be the weather harsh or sunny,
shooters seldom spurn bounding bunnies.

Hares have mastered great deceptions
running their broken-field misdirection.

Just kick up a cottontail bounder
and they'll more likely circle 'round ya.

If you shoot'm good you must concur
they're best served up as Hasenpfeffer.

Letchworth State Park
Genesee River
Castile, NY

Keepers

It's not the sweetness of the chocolate
or the tartness of the lime,
It's the titillation of the pallet
that makes tasting so divine.

It's not the grandeur of the sunset,
nor the allure of foreign lands,
The knowledge that you've been there
Is what your paltry life demands.

It's not the vastness of the oceans
but the crystal clarity of the brook,
That determines thirst is slackening
with that long last sip that you took.

It's not the brilliant gifts of Handel
or endless beauty of Nature's songs,
It's the welcome or the warning
that lets you know that you belong.

It's not the raff of your connections
nor your most impressive social gain,
It's the love and depth of friendship
that at day's end you still retain.

It's not the length of earthly journey
that dictates what might have been,
But how wisely you applied the time
securing peace that rests within.

It's not good deeds or cash donations
or what pilgrim's path you've trod,
It's the truths embedded in your heart
while traversing your last towards God.

Posted

The Master's envelopes are flinty seed pods
that He posts to us each year,
sowing a promise of the future
suggesting a bounty in times near.

tucked inside's a guarded message
on how the new dawn shall proceed,
seeds struggle seeking new life
amongst plowed furrows and roadside weeds.

many kernels fall on fertile ground
where they root and vigorously grow,
with ample portions providing sustenance
that all birds and beasts need so.

some come to rest on rock-ribbed ground
with which they can't abide,
they're dried to dust providing loam
where next year's seeds'll hide.

no pods are ever turned away
some'll rest one hundred years,
for each there is a purpose,
for each a calling clear.

My Mom
Anna T. Hellmann
1919 - Three Years of Age

Annie

It's hard to recall
a day that her life didn't intersect mine.

This self-effacing plain woman
had survived the Great Depression,
a lack of formal education,
and two World Wars.

As Carl's loving wife and partner in life,
she was by choice low maintenance
and clan driven.

Uncontested family matriarch,
this formidable lady shamed today's shallow copies
and gender confused biddies.

This woman's strengths and her sense of history
were lovingly grafted
into our family's growth rings.

She expanded my world
with Shel Silverstein's poetry,
and an uncompromising German work ethic
that stressed a rather foreign concept – responsibility.

Upon her knee
I learned respect for all.

Annie's faith was simple and deep.
She showed me the footprints of Jesus,
and the tranquility of nature.

Friendships spanned miles and generations;
all yet require a century to outlive.

Through simple acts of love
Annie changed destinies,
and nurtured those that the world had given up.

The gift that I cherished most
was that she called me Son.

Storm Damage

Like a jilted lover that just has posted
a heart rending message to Dear John,
in a storm of tears and blowing fury
nature has bid mankind be gone.

Katrina's windy thrusts exposed our vitals
laying open a hidden rotting core,
exposing old transgressions and abuses
we addressed some forty years before.

It's not all the billions that's required
or the grief in gathering up our dead,
but our failure after years trying
we're still two nations, not one instead.

We can put the cities back together
and engineers can redirect great waterways,
but it's apparent we've not figured out
how to blend colors yet today.

After years legislating what's considered equal
setting quotas to redivide the national wealth,
yet we failed to change the hearts of men
and I confess it includes myself.

Civilization's veneer has been storm eroded
exposing the ugly beast that lurks inside,
let's consign our hyphenations to the melting pot
so that only Americans will here reside.

In the early morning hours of 8/29/05 hurricane Katrina crashed ashore with 145mph winds as a Class #4 storm in Biloxi, Miss. On 8/30/05 three breaches occurred in the New Orleans levy system flooding 80 percent of the city.

Along The Way

In circumspect, we question if
we said things right or bungled it?

We rue the times when we've lashed out,
to dismiss poor souls with curse or shout.

Were the challenged offered equal chance,
or sacrificed because of patience scant?

Just how well did intent succeed?
Did we stand with friends in times of need?

Did we capture much of valued worth,
or advance the cause of peace on earth?

Were our gifts enough to feed the poor?
 Did we welcome all who sought our door?

Unpolished truths learned along the way,
await some time hence ... perhaps today.

Carp Catchers
Dan Pittman (L) and Ralph Burnstine (R)
Dr. L.J. Darr Memorial Wetland

Frogtown

In the deltas east of Frogtown
on Lake Erie's southern shore,
remains a trace of ancient marsh men
whose souls reflect what ran before.

Fiercely protective of their bloodlines
that first faced the Iroquois,
casting seeds amongst the Black Swamp
that modern progress would destroy.

From grim marsh they scratched a living,
fin and Feather was their crop,
trapping profits in their fur farms
and praying the old ways wouldn't stop.

But times changed and German farmers
drained the swamps and planted grain,
all's now modern and efficient
but frontier spirit still remains.

Diagnosis

Impaled and raised upon the lance of fear.

Not the end envisioned in youth,
not the glorious death of a reluctant warrior,
or the heroic choice of happenstance.
Just a regretful gruesome crumbling
witnessed by a scabbed-over surface
of ancient ills.
Ten years of going the wrong way,
aging, not growing
this miraculous shell.
The trauma of body parts
separated, smashed, or reduced.
The stunning silence of organs
that fail their design.
Misplacing of well defined wit,
and only fleeting memories of sharp senses.
The Years of Gold flow to lead
when illnesses are encountered
that were previously assigned only to others.
A moment of stark realization
that has come home to roost.

Embrace the fear.

Dr. Granny

I've seen scads of somber saw-bones,
In years past more than a few,
I've sent with pride three sons to Harvard,
All were kids of physicians that I knew.

With sharp needles they poked and prodded,
Each orifice checked 'round and through,
I became reluctant subject for redundant testing,
Sure vampires gorged on blood they drew.

Challenging the bounds of modern medicine
By contracting ailments rarely seen before,
Procuring skills to digest the master billings
And finally realize healers don't get poor.

In the end you're pressed to wonder
If Granny's down-home healing wasn't best,
Just swill rye whiskey adrip'n dolloped honey,
And gobs of Vapor Rub'll get the rest.

Blue Flag
Dr. LJ Darr Memorial Wetland
Oak Harbor, OH

Awakening

Locked in crimson promise of poppy's petals
    And the velvet hue of tulip buds,
        Is the assurance of life's resurgence
            With the arrival of Springtime floods.

On each breath of warming currents
    From retreating Winter's breeze,
        New growth gathers on the branches
            Of stark, barren sleeping trees.

As hidden secrets of impending Spring
    Are exposed to Winter waifs,
        Earth's stirrings of the new found life
            Raise the sleeping denizens of this place.

There's a flushing of each blade of grass
    That stretches from disabling sleep,
        Forming lush lanes of thatch a poppin'
            In verdant padding 'neath our feet.

Audible sighs from buds awakened
    In the flora of the plains,
        Producing species so abundant
            It defies recall of their names.

Each year this passion of the living
    Enraptures all the world around,
        Enthralled we sit and ponder
            As the Maker's miracles abound.

Progress?

Yankees now reflect upon youth at seventy-seven,
Year forty-five braced life's terminus ere a century ago.
Science's success finally has met the longevity test,
And it comes up wanting in life quality ya know?

Are all codgers mentally sharp and real sprightly?
Or Botox altered with unsightly wrinkles removed?
Will they be hip to eschewing entanglements' grip,
And with blue pills have hot sex that's approved?

Some fools think they might now live forever,
Desperate to grasp at promises writ only in sand.
A long life's the great hope 'mongst most timid folk,
But I'll not abandon my full life that's grand.

Afternoon Surprise
Dr. LJ Darr Memorial Wetland
Oak Harbor, OH

Billy Buck

I've seen you on the Summer days
As balmy breeze on winds do play.

Come opening day will you be found
In common haunts upon this ground?

Will we meet in death on uphill spines
Down wind from beds where does recline?

Should I hang above your well used scrapes
To guarantee the choice prize I'll take?

Must I search each day the master trail
That'll slow your tracks in great detail?

Can I mask my scent upon the winds
And lure you in as rut begins?

Deer tag's been bought and license signed
It could be better yet if you showed this time!

Bargain

I seize upon next stumbling breath,
And hope last pill will give me rest.

Obsessing with most mundane things
To augur what this life-change brings.

Most times unwell, depressed, and sad;
Short trips through hell can be quite bad.

Some lust for wealth, great looks, or vice;
Just take this pain – give back my life.

The Kiss

Angry clouds engorged with seas of wet
Streak serrated sullen sky.

Valkyries in quest of Summer's best
Fleeing Winter's gathering scythe.

To stand aghast as thunderheads pass
At surreal pace they rumble by.

Imparting great fear to all creatures near,
As lance lightening rents blackness nigh.

The flora below bob and bow in great show
All that's rigid will meet its demise.

All life bends low in humble fealty show
Hugging earth to offer prayers and mute cries.

Raging storm will have its way and linger,
Destructive deluge tarries not to compromise.

It blows a moist kiss without none can exist
After lover's passion there's calm and goodbye.

Nesting Geese
Dr. LJ Darr Memorial Wetland
Oak Harbor, OH

Connubial Conversation

      Just tell me, my dear, don't show me,
All my foibles and failures you see,
      With my errant conscience in constant denial
Avoiding the consequences of life that I flee.

      Complaints aren't construed as constructive
And crystal logic won't lessen the bite.
      That's a ploy to hush timid and trusting,
But we scoundrels'll get it 'fore other folks might.

      Waste no time on remorse or great anguish,
Play out the hand 'til reality hits.
      Calmly inform me what all's required
And I'll tell you if I might ever fit.

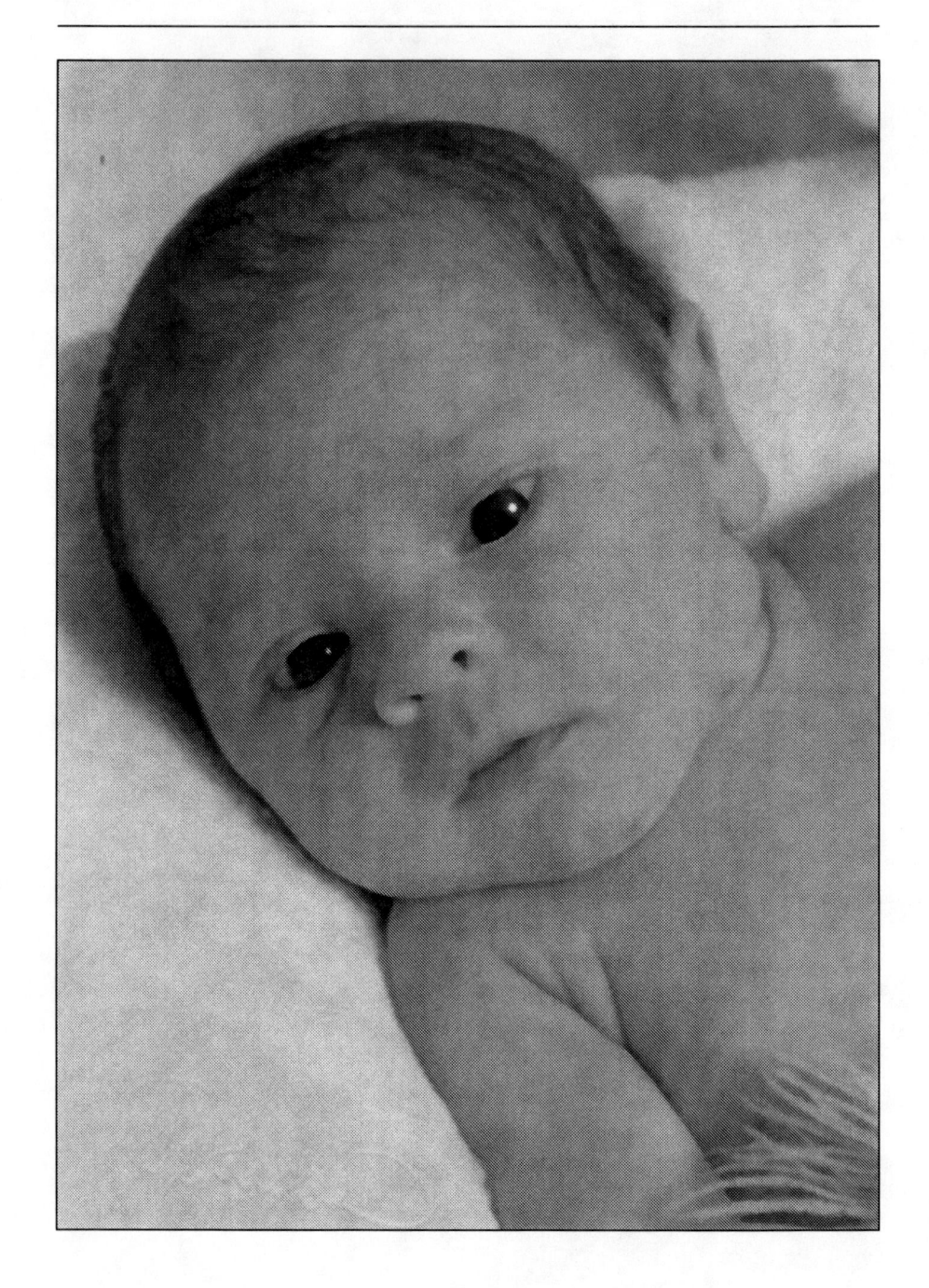

Kole
First Grandson

Branch

A miracle plucked
 from the limb of life.
Spellbinding mystery of creation,
 a child's birth,
  a linage continued,
   a grandson!

Each generation awaits this seminal event.
A reaffirmation of forbearers
 long since forgotten,
  that now dwell in the present.

Grow strong in grace and wisdom Kole,
 inhale fortitude and devour life.
Rejoice in the light and revere the truth.
In Nature
 behold the face of God.

Destiny will whisper your name.

From Opa to:
Kole Steven Hellmann
Born: February 17, 2006

Silent Shadow

*With fluid strength and fragile beauty
Akin to an opening night's ballet,
A red-tailed hawk rides changing updrafts
With impressive skill and great display.*

*Graceful raptor ranged the switch-grass
That inundates the land around,
His approach assumes a rambling glide
In suspended flight o'er rushing ground.*

*Delicate wing tips curl gently upward,
As protruding digits rake heavens nigh,
His bristling neck band boasts its shackles
As beak-crowned head cuts virgin sky.*

*His approach in utter silence
Can't be discerned from placid breeze,
And the whispering death he deftly renders
Comes from heaven above the trees.*

As willing witness to this dance of death
That's choreographed o'er killing fields,
The last act is done with the final plunge
As beneath clenched talons the quarry yields.

The majesty of raptor's trappings
And the regal bearing he displays,
Cloaks the devastation of the hunted
That visits this placid sun-drenched day.

At Nine

Loren is a Southern Bell,
from mellow accent you can tell.

Raised on up in Tennessee,
as cute as frog-spit she can be.

A country girl with coquette's eyes,
as years pass by she'll wow the guys.

She fields softballs with speed and grace,
and smacks fast pitches coming over the plate.

Wise in ways beyond her years,
she banishes with spunk her girlish fears.

Her heart is pure and smile's wide,
she long has been her Mother's pride.

She'll do quite well in years to come,
great promise grows best in fortune's sun.

Love from Opa

Sum Total

*Lovers
color their world
in half truths and transparent designs.*

*Deceptively
sculpting the banality of reality,
and the tortured lessons of time.*

*Venturing all
to weave a world
that rails against calamity and pain.*

*In the end,
efforts exceed expectations
and only fond memories remain.*

Mallard Moments
Huntington Valley, PA

Thrash'n

My clock is set for half-past four
with decoy bags stacked by the door.

Good friends with dogs still wait for me
in hopes of times that used to be.

But my body's melded to my bed,
exhaustion dares me raise my head.

Awake I am, thoughts working grand,
but the flesh declines the mind's demands.

The cancer's ills have won this day
for on this rack I'm forced to stay.

When hunting for some duck I'd winged
this game I'd play in capturing.

I'd stand far off and give him ground,
'till his life's used up from thrash'n 'round.

When will gave out and no life shown,
I'd close the gap and take him home.

(1st day, 2nd half of duck season, 2004)

Fruits of Morpheus

*Levitate
this racked and tortured frame
into the dusk.*

*Beguile
the minions of sleep and release.*

*With ease
free the gnarled fist
so to join
the ballet of motion and ease.*

*The mind
once cruelly anchored to
this millstone of pain
slips the tether.*

*But Morpheus,
you are a strumpet
that haggles too well
and accepts only total fealty.*

*Reluctantly,
I refuse thy favors.*

Political Planting

The Winter crop of November 2, 2004.

Again, to plant
the seed corn of liberty.

Will the seedbed be faithfully prepared,
or is the ground only rough plowed
leaving hard clods?

In planting
will we choose to conservatively drill the seed,
or liberally broadcast it?

Both planting techniques
claim a full harvest of democracy.

Will the venture glean
the heady profits of a free market,
or the meager portions of the commune?

What we choose to plant this political season
is what we will surely reap.

Looking For The Season
Katie At The Darr

Duck Watch

Scattered remnants of the hunting day
Float above the marshland mews,
In those moments that proceed the night
Weary hunters sense it's through.

At day's end they stand at ready
For roost-bound ducks that rush the night,
Shooters may have luck to catch'm
Filling their bag limits with delight.

Waterfowl display an uncanny sixth sense
Determining when shooting hours come and go,
Hunters swear the birds wear watches
For they leave early and come back very slow.

But puntmen pray the clouds'll roil up
Blurring weak sun at dawn and dusk,
Skittish dabblers become less cautious
And offer hunters more birds to bust.

It's the first and last half hour
That'll tempt most the ducks to fly,
It's when waterfowlers of the marshland
Give those greenheads one last try.

Swallow On Duck Box
Dr. L.J Darr Memorial Wetland

God's Face

We stand in awe of sunset's grandeur
Or marvel at frail fleeting birds,
Yet some fools deny their Maker
With mundane reasoning that's absurd.

All around are God's creations
In earth's resplendent tapestry,
When we think we've hit the limit,
He'll reveal much more to see.

We must take the time to notice
Those extra minutes we must dare.
Each breath reveals the face of God,
All creation shows He cares.

Twilight at the Marsh
Winter night at Darr Wetland

Good Times

It's on the puntman's side of midnight
when duckmen flock to warm-up warrens.
A dusky Nubian night blots out visible lights,
save the portal beacon from our ramshackle barn.

Ponds crack in the vise of the newly made ice
scattering sunshine suitors at Nature's behest.
And those who remain are adjudged quite insane
for they venture all for the waterfowl quest.

But big ducks won't arrive 'til the temperatures dive
and the mellow green colors of Summer have fled.
So we'll set here and freeze, water up to our knees,
hoping dawn's dabblers soon arrive to be bled.

At first light they come, and it's already done,
before worn old waders give up my dry gear.
And nuts it may be, but these good times ain't free,
sure on the morrow you'll find me right here.

Bird Dog
Kurt's Dog Drake

It's The Truth!

All hunters tell the grandest lies,
They're blarney blessed and humble guys.

If shooter's game bag's slim today,
You'll hear tall tales of the "Got Aways".

While play'n cards in deer camp snug,
Last year's "Almost" makes Pope & Young.

If duckmen's dogs did all they said,
The whole Third World'd be overfed.

Those 'coon dog guys stay out all night,
Did they bag their game or just get tight?

A gobbler hunter's best disguise
Is to lie'n wait 'til a bird struts by.

But the greatest lie of the whole damn bunch,
Is I missed you sweetie ...
and I'll be home for lunch.

Mull Covered Bridge
Built 1851
Sandusky County, OH

From Here To There

  Life offers us conundrums
that are often couched in fear,
Unaware just how far we've come,
and unsure where to go from here.

  It's a perilous path to follow
unexplored since distant youth,
When each day was fast and furious,
when mind and soul were real footloose.

  Ignoring risks that might prove fatal
in our mindless quest of middle age,
In high times of slaying dragons,
advancing plans that we had made.

  But in the twilight of the later years
when the traveler's sight grows dim,
We'll stumble on some memory
of how it once had been.

  When searching for direction
that we had previously displayed,
We expose knowledge gaps and obfuscations
that render logic false and frayed.

All mankind eventually gets there
just at different points in time,
It's apparent we lack protection
from life's nagging truths sublime.

Still to find are boundless treasures
for each day's a blessed gift,
So present to those around you
a strong heart and pleasant wit.

Navigate into the current,
let the sails catch rushing winds,
Search out and seize the moment
and work on things that might have been.

Sssnake

Slithering slimy scaly snake,
get off this path
that I must take.

Shimmering scooter sally south,
find another marsh
to make your house.

Silent slim-lined silhouette,
take all your kids;
aren't you gone yet?

Saunter on the simmering street,
with an ounce of luck
my truck you'll meet.

Oakwood Cemetery
Veteran's Section
Fremont, OH

Bedrock

      From promontory to far horizon
lays a vast expanse
of thrashing sea.
      Liquid corridors
traveled by the messengers of Mars,
that have strewn upon rough-hewn shores
shark-finned columns of granite
nestled in high tides of green blades.
      Each monolith uniformly addressed with
a record of a life cut short,
a soldier sent,
a son or daughter's sacrifice.
      Flag draped bedrock,
stiffening the foundations of liberty.
      Upon these strong stilled shoulders
firmly rests the Republic.

Silver Dowry

Upon forest floor the annual gathering
Of frost withered leafy palms,
That in Summer blithely beckoned
From silver maple groves beyond.

Resilient stems that turned the many
Graceful gesturing velvet hands,
Would display their silver linings
When storm clouds threatened forest stands.

The flowing veins that once had offered
A photosynthetic greening life,
On cool winds have turned quite ridged
To become Fall's flapping leather kites.

They release their grip of engaged lips
From beloved branches that they hold,
To whisper secrets of the season's end
That has long since been foretold.

Prostrate before their maple masters
Cloaked in earth tones of loss and sorrow,
These fallen sentinels of the wooded glade
In silent moments await the morrow.

Giving homage to expanding roots
Becoming one with waiting clay,
Insuring century's stand of maple giants
Paying resurrection's passage in coming days.

Saint Hubert's Bounty
Dr. L.J. Darr Memorial Wetland

Shrine of the Miraculous Wing Shot

  Decoys stand as patient acolytes
In the grass circle that I'd chopped,
Once knee deep in wheat and prairie grass
That was sown for cover crop.
  In the quiet of the goose field
I attend to Sunrise Mass,
Ever thankful to the Master
By recalling great hunts of recent past.
  I donned the vestments of the Deacon,
A layered wetland camouflage,
Which denotes the Monks of Waterfowling
From the Most Holy Hunter's Lodge.
  With fluted reed I summon supplicants
From the far corners of the marsh,
They'll descend on wings of angels
If the calling's not too harsh.
  They flock in search of last communion
With their plastic brethren on the ground,
To genuflect upon the cut grass field
As the wrath of Remington smites them down.
  The stilled geese are Saint Hubert's bounty,
Offerings from ancient patron of hunter's lore,
So we'll all expect to see you Sunday next
Here at the Church of the Great Outdoors.

John "Lucky" Kronauge
Winner of the Whitetails Unlimited Gun of the Year

Mr. Lucky

      Our Club sponsors sportsmen's banquets
at the American Legion hall that's near.
      Where deer hunters from the counties 'round
gathered for hearty victuals and free beer.

      The food will titillate your palate
and the booze has been known to flow,
      Propelled on the waves of bids and raffles
guests gain in animation as their cash stash goes.

      I usually work the door-side booth
with my daughter's betrothed John,
      Hawking gun dreams at cut-rate possession
before dwindling raffle ticket stocks are gone.

      This year John's real world job commitments
insured that he could not get away,
      But feeling lucky he sent raffle money
to purchase all the gun tickets he could play.

      I plunked down three brand new twenties –
first from Kristy, then John, then me
      To garner Gun of the Year from Whitetails,
a sequentially numbered 300 mag. Weatherby.

Late that night when I reached my house
the daughter asked how my luck had run,
    It took her time before she really fathomed
she held the ticket that took that coveted gun.

    Excitement soon overwhelmed her
knowing that she could gift her John the gun,
    I gratefully survived the great temptation
to let ominous omission construe what's done.

    But to find some way to best describe
my conflicted feelings at day's end,
    It's as if compelled to watch the IRS
confiscated your prize Mercedes Benz.

All

In the wilderness of glen or field
All struggles must sustain, not yield.

Wild creatures' premier sense is flight,
When cornered conjure up great might.

The horse will run until its dead,
Smart beasts like men will use their heads.

Which is more wise, the man or horse?
Human beings promote the altered course.

Pray God I pass the way I lived,
With soul and mind no more to give.

Pied-billed Grebe
Dr. L.J. Darr Memorial Wetland

Keep'n Track

    Special season tips my limits
of the Blue and Green-Winged Teal,
        But to pass up Wood Duck not in season
dampens a hunter's morning zeal.

    I busted many Canadas,
both the Lesser and the Great,
        Quite often for my dinner
'twas Gads and Mallards that I ate.

    I took a toll of streaking Pintails
and downed some skittish Redhead Duck,
        I filled the bill with windblown Goldeneye
and bobbin' Bufflehead out of luck.

    I'll admit to nailing Ruddy Ducks
for no apparent hunting gain,
        Perturbed at missing swooping Baldpates
that had fled my faulty aim.

    To the taxidermist for a standing mount
went a Merganser, one Hooded male,
        But I ignored his many cousins
since their meat reeks of fish entrails.

      I got a brace of Shovelers
and a Ross's Goose with best of luck,
      But had a terrible time deciphering
'tween Blue Bill and Ringneck Duck.

      Logged in some passing Black Duck
and a couple wandering Snows,
      The tally of the waterfowl
depends on how the weather goes.

      In years past there's a big bay duck
I've never really tracked,
      So I'm changing up old decoy sets
and I'll rig for Canvasback.

      When the game bag's tasted all the species
that Lake Erie's inland marshes do provide,
      I'll move once more to Jersey's eastern shore
to take sea ducks as they coast by.

Nirvana

When not pursuing wild game,
spectator sports are what remain.
Sportsmen oft' succumb to gear addictions,
from Cabela treks that scout conditions.
With sniper's eyes they'll soon affix
endless treasure troves of log and brick.

New fangled gear and fabled guides
crowd themed lodges where the loot resides.
Every gun, and bow, and fishing rod;
each boat, decoy, and boot that's trod.
Never short of shell, or slug, or hook,
nor carcass of the game what's took.
Many tie-in sales and slick arrays,
with live fish tanks and pool displays.

The Bargain Cave's close to my heart
'tis where most fabled hunts'll start.
And if I'm not found afield today,
I've clinched a deal up Dundee way.

As One
Geese Headed South

Living Hues

Come stroll with me on dawn drenched beach,
    to recall those times now out of reach.
To speak of things we both hold dear,
    in familiar terms for each other's ears.
Come hike with me on woodland trails
    between spiked pines and dogwoods frail.
We'll climb to heights where few have been
    and commune with woodland denizens.
Come perch with me on cliff face high,
    amongst peaks impaled on cotton sky.
Come wade with me through a pristine brook
    that meanders 'round hidden forest nook.
Come slog with me on upland dikes,
    in bog bottoms where the ducks alight.
Come repose as ebony night enfolds,
    before morn's vapored mists flee sunlight bold.
Nature deftly paints an image of what our soul is like,
    choose only vibrant colors; eschew the black and white.

For Nancy

Toussaint Swans
Dr. LJ Darr Memorial Wetland

Eternity

    ...is a familiar hunt
that has bagged its limit,
with a closing day unanticipated.
    a season grown to legend
consumed by the lake,
the wood,
the marsh,
and the prairie grass.
    a metamorphosis of insipient youth
into grizzled graybeard
comfortably expounding upon a worn davenport
    in a monotonous litany
of the good times,
the bad times,
the fast times,
and ultimately,
    the lack of...

Season's Limit

In the ode of the hunter
each line is a memory,
each verse a season,
and each poem an adventure harvested.
    Life becomes the game bag of the soul.